SECOND EDITION

3

LET'S GO

Student Book

Karen Frazier

Ritsuko Nakata

Barbara Hoskins

Steve Wilkinson

with songs by Carolyn Graham

OXFORD
UNIVERSITY PRESS

Icons

Let's Go Student Book 3 consists of eight units, with a review section after every two units. Every unit is divided into five lessons. Each lesson is identified by a colorful icon. The same icons are used for reference on the corresponding pages in both the *Workbook* and the *Teacher's Book.*

Let's Talk
Functional dialogue

Let's Sing or Let's Chant
Interactive song or chant based on the new grammatical structure

Let's Learn
New grammatical structure

Let's Listen
Listening test and unit review

Let's Read
Reading skills development

Let's Review
Further review after every two units

Table of Contents

Let's Talk

Excuse me. Where's the lunchroom?

It's across from the gym. Come with me.

OK.

My name is Amy. What's your name?

I'm David.

These are my friends, Ben and Wendy. This is David.

Hi, David.

Excuse me. Where's the lunchroom?
It's across from the gym.

Ask and answer.

Where's the library?

It's | across from the office.
     | next to the lunchroom.

across from

next to

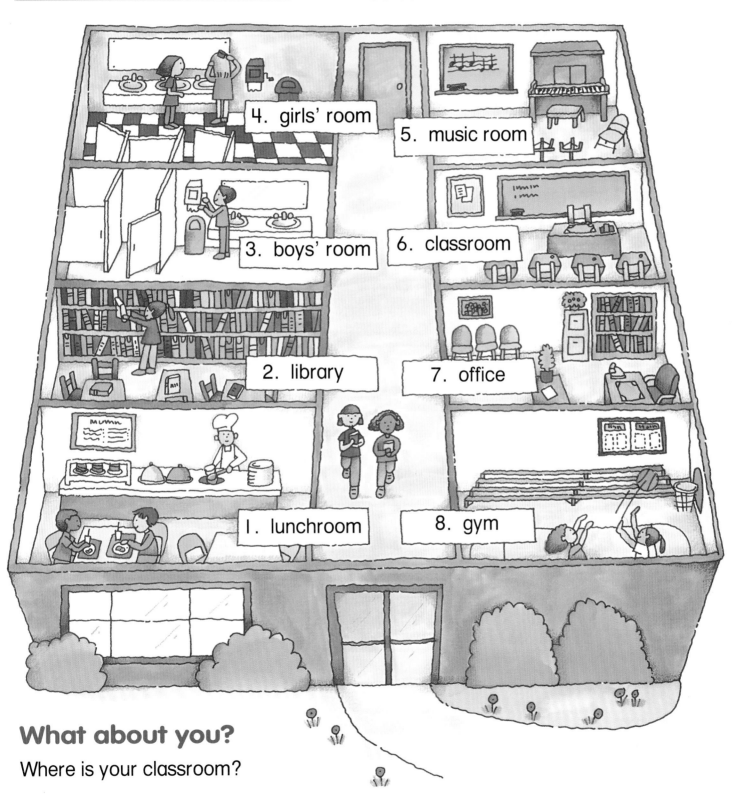

4. girls' room

5. music room

3. boys' room

6. classroom

2. library

7. office

1. lunchroom

8. gym

What about you?

Where is your classroom?

Amy's in the music room.
She's playing the piano.

David and Wendy are in the classroom.
They're watching a video.

Ask and answer.

Where is	he? she?
He's She's	in the library.

Where are they?

They're in the lunchroom.

1.

2.

3.

4.

5.

6.

Play a game. Ask and answer.

What's | he | doing?
       | she |

He's | reading.
She's |

What are they doing?

They're swimming.

Numbers

1. Read and say the numbers.

eleven

twelve

thirteen

fourteen

fifteen

sixteen

seventeen

eighteen

nineteen

twenty

2. Count from twenty to thirty.

3. Count by tens to one hundred.

10

20

30

40

50

60

70

80

90

100

Sounds and Sentences

classroom

glass

clock

glue

clean

glove

Please clean the clock in the classroom.

There is glue on this glass and this glove.

♪ Where's Roy? ♪

Where's Roy?
　In the lunchroom.
　He's in the lunchroom.
Where?
　In the lunchroom.
　There, in the lunchroom.
Who's in the lunchroom?
　Roy's in the lunchroom.
　He's in the lunchroom now.

Where's Tim?
　In the gym.
　He's there, in the gym.
Where's Kim?
　In the gym.
　She's there with him.
　He's there with her.
　She's there with him.
　They're there in the gym right now.

Unit 1

Let's Listen

True or false? Listen and check.

1. ☐ True ☐ False   2. ☐ True ☐ False   3. ☐ True ☐ False

4. ☐ True ☐ False   5. ☐ True ☐ False   6. ☐ True ☐ False

Listen and circle the number.

1. 15   50   2. 13   30

3. 17   70   4. 12   20

5. 19   90   6. 18   80

7. 14   40   8. 16   60

Let's Talk

Do you want some?
    Yes, please.
    No, thanks.

Ask and answer.

> What do you have?
> I have some paper.

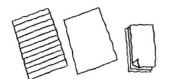
1. paper

2. chalk

3. tape

4. ribbon

5. glue

6. paint

7. string

8. scissors

Yes or no?

> Do you have any paper?
> Yes, I do.
> No, I don't.

What about you?

I have some _____.

Ben has some paint. He doesn't have any string.

Amy and Wendy have some string, but they don't have any paint.

We have some string, and you have some paint.

Let's share!

Make sentences.

She has some _____.
She doesn't have any _____.

They have some _____.
They don't have any _____.

Ask and answer.

What does | he | have?
         | she |

He | has some chalk.
She |

What do they have?

They have some tape.

Yes or no? Ask questions about the picture above.

Does | he | have any tape?
     | she |

Yes, | he | does.
     | she |

No, | he | doesn't.
    | she |

Do they have any glue?

Yes, they do.

No, they don't.

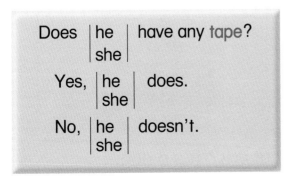

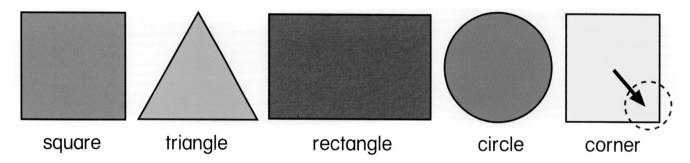

| square | triangle | rectangle | circle | corner |

A Paper Dog

1. Fold the paper and make a triangle.

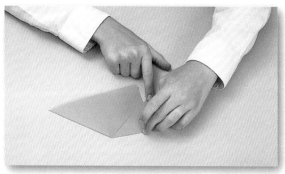

2. Fold this corner. This is an ear.

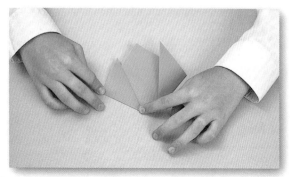

3. Fold this corner. This is an ear, too.

4. Fold this corner. This is a nose.

5. Draw two circles. These are eyes.

6. What is it? It's a dog.

Read and answer.

1. Does the boy have any scissors?
2. What does he have?
3. What is he making?

Sounds and Sentences

play

black

plate

blue

airplane

blow

Play with the airplane. Don't play with the plate.

Blow up the black balloon and the blue balloon.

Let's Sing

♪ **Sue Doesn't Have Any Glue** ♪

Sue doesn't have any glue.
Sue doesn't have any glue.
  Sue has some paper.
  Sue has some string.
  Sue has a bird and it's learning to sing.
Sue has some ribbon.
Sue has some chalk.
Sue has a dog and it's learning to talk.
  But Sue isn't happy, no she's feeling blue,
  Sue doesn't have any glue, (boo hoo)
  Sue doesn't have any glue.

16

Let's Listen

Listen and circle.

1.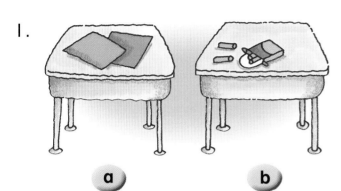

   a   b

2.

   a   b

3.

   a   b

4.

   a   b

Yes or no? Listen and check.

1. ☐ Yes, they do. ☐ No, they don't. 2. ☐ Yes, he does. ☐ No, he doesn't.

3. ☐ Yes, she does. ☐ No, she doesn't. 4. ☐ Yes, they do. ☐ No, they don't.

Let's Review

A. Say and act.

1.

_____. Where's the lunchroom?

It's across from the gym.

_____.

OK.

2.

I have some green paper. _____?

Yes, please.

Here you are.

_____.

B. Ask your partner.

Do you have any _____?

	string	paint	chalk	scissors	glue	tape
Yes						
No						

C. Answer the question.

What do you have?

D. Listen and circle.

1. a   b

2. a   b

3. a   b

4. a   b

E. Listen and read.

1. My school has   twenty   teachers.
                     twelve

2. There are   fifteen   students in the gym.
                 fifty

3. The library is   across from   the music room.
                      next to

4. The gym is across from the   office.
                                  classroom.

Let's Talk

Can you play with us tomorrow?
Sorry, I can't. I'm busy.
Yes, I can. I'm free.

Ask and answer.

> What do you do on Monday?
>   I go to art class.

1. art class

2. English class

3. piano class

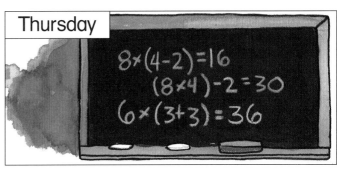

4. math class

5. swimming class

6. computer class

What about you?

Do you go to school on Sunday?
Do you watch TV on Sunday?
Do you do homework on Sunday?

After school David does his homework.
Then he studies English.

Every day Amy sings at school.
After school she practices the piano.

After school Ben and Wendy play soccer.
On Saturday they play tennis.

I/We/They	He/She
do	does
go	goes
play	plays
practice	practices
sing	sings
study	studies
take	takes
watch	watches

Ask and answer.

What does | he | do after school?
         | she |

He | watches TV.
She |

What do they do after school?

They play outside.

1. watch TV

2. take a nap

3. play outside

4. go to the bookstore

5. play video games

6. practice the piano

Yes or no? Ask questions about the pictures above.

Does | he | take a nap after school?
     | she |

Yes, | he | does.
       | she |

No, | he | doesn't.
     | she |

Do they watch TV after school?

Yes, they do.

No, they don't.

Favorite Day

This is Linda. Her favorite day is Saturday. She plays basketball with her father.

This is Dan. His favorite day is Tuesday. He goes to karate class with his sister.

This is Jack. His favorite day is Sunday. He stays home and watches TV with his dog.

Read and answer.

1. What is Linda's favorite day?
2. What does Dan do on Tuesday?
3. Does Jack stay home on Sunday?

Sounds and Sentences

present

brother

prince

brown

princess

brush

The princess is giving a present to the prince.

My brother is brushing his brown hair.

Let's Sing

♪ Busy, Busy, Busy ♪

Busy, busy, busy every day.
Busy, busy, busy, I can't play.
Are you busy Monday?
  Yes, I am.
  English classes, music classes
Monday, Tuesday, Wednesday, Thursday.
Are you busy Friday?
  Yes, I am.
  Friday is a busy day.
Are you busy Saturday?
Can you play?
  No! Saturday's a very, very busy day.
Busy, busy, busy, I can't play.
I'm busy, busy every day.
  But not on Sunday!
  Sunday is my free day
  And I can play!

Let's Listen

Yes or no? Listen and check.

	Monday	Tuesday	Wednesday	Thursday	Friday

1. ☐ Yes, she does.
   ☐ No, she doesn't.

2. ☐ Yes, she does.
   ☐ No, she doesn't.

3. ☐ Yes, she does.
   ☐ No, she doesn't.

4. ☐ Yes, she is.
   ☐ No, she isn't.

Listen and circle.

1.

   a   b

2.

   a   b

3.
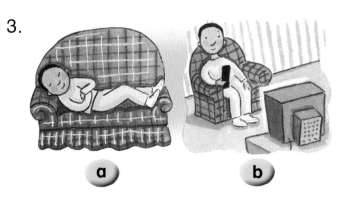

   a   b

4.

   a   b

Let's Talk

I'm sorry I'm late.
That's OK.

What time is it?

3:15
It's three fifteen.

3:30
It's three thirty.

3:45
It's three forty-five.

4:00
It's four o'clock.

Ask and answer.

When does	he	get up?
	she	
He	gets up at 6:30.	
She		

When do they go to school?

They go to school at 8:15.

1. 6:30

2. 12:45

3. 8:15

4. 9:45

5. 6:00

6. 7:30

What about you?

When do you eat dinner?

	Monday	Tuesday	Wednesday	Thursday	Friday

Ben **always** rides his bike to school.

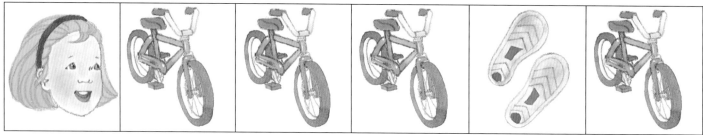

Wendy **usually** rides her bike to school.

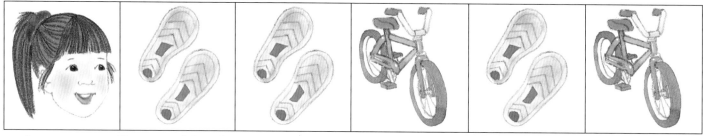

Amy **sometimes** rides her bike to school.

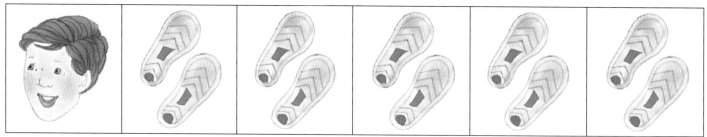

David **never** rides his bike to school. He always walks.

always	= 100%
usually	= 80%
sometimes	= 40%
never	= 0%

Yes or no?

Does	he / she	ever eat pizza?

Yes,	he / she	always / usually / sometimes	eats pizza.

No,	he / she	never eats pizza.

Do they ever watch TV?

Yes, they	always / usually / sometimes	watch TV.

No, they never watch TV.

1. sometimes

2. usually

3. always

4. never

5. usually

6. never

What about you?

Do you ever play tag?
Do you ever take a nap?
Do you ever sleep outside?

Let's Read

Jeff's Busy Day

Jeff is very busy every day.
He goes to school early in the morning.

After school he rides his bicycle.

Sometimes he plays soccer with his friends.

He usually eats dinner with his family.

Then they watch TV.

He always does his homework in the evening.

He goes to sleep at 10:00 every night.

Read and answer.

1. When does Jeff go to school?
2. Does he ever play soccer after school?
3. What does he do in the evening?
4. What time does he go to sleep?

Sounds and Sentences

train

draw

tree

dress

truck

drum

The train and the truck are near a tree.

Can you draw a dress and a drum?

♪ **Three Fifteen** ♪

3:15.
A quarter after three.
3:15.
A quarter after three.
    What time is it?
    Please tell me.
It's fifteen minutes after three.

8:15.
A quarter after eight.
8:15.
A quarter after eight.
    What time is it?
    Are we late?
It's fifteen minutes after eight.

10:15.
A quarter after ten.
10:15.
A quarter after ten.
Let's all sing this song again.
It's fifteen minutes after ten.

Let's Listen

Listen and circle the time.

1. 12:30   1:00

2. 5:45   6:15

3. 6:45   7:15

4. 10:00   10:30

Listen and check.

1. Do they ever wake up at 6:30?

	David	Amy	Wendy	Ben
always				
usually	✔			
sometimes				
never				

2. Do they ever eat pizza for lunch?

	David	Amy	Wendy	Ben
always				
usually				
sometimes				
never				

Let's Review

A. Say and act.

1.

Can you play with us tomorrow?

Sorry, I can't. _____.

_____?

Sunday's OK. I'm free.

2.

_____?

It's 5:45.

Oh, no! I'm late. Bye!

_____.

_____.

That's OK.

B. Ask your partner.

Do you ever _____ on Sunday?

	Yes			No
	always	usually	sometimes	never
do homework				
watch TV				
get up early				
go to the bookstore				

C. Answer the question.

What do you do every Saturday?

D. Listen and circle.

1.
   a   b

2.
   a   b

3.
   a   b

4.
   a   b

E. Listen and read.

1. Ben and Wendy go to computer class on   Tuesday. / Thursday.

2. Amy always goes to art class at   9:15. / 8:45.

3. David   sometimes / usually   plays soccer after school.

4. Ben never   gets up early / does homework   on Sunday.

Do you mean this one?
  Yes, I do.
  No, the big one.

Ask and answer.

> Which hat do you like?
> I like the red one.

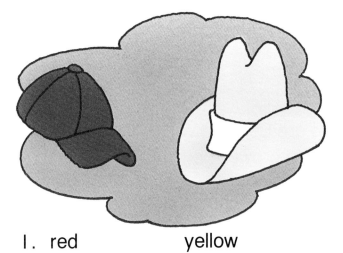

1. red   yellow

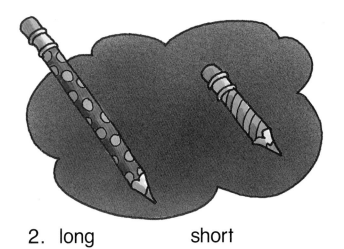

2. long   short

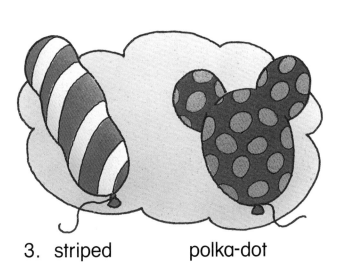

3. striped   polka-dot

4. old   new

5. thick   thin

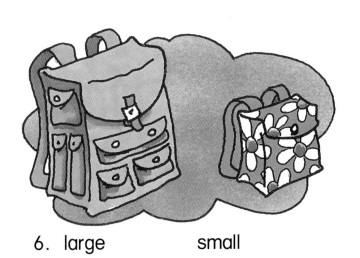

6. large   small

Let's Learn

This is Amy. She's wearing a polka-dot dress. It's red and white.

Here are Ben and Wendy. They're wearing brown shorts and striped shirts.

Here they are again. Thank you, boys and girls!

More Clothes

a coat   a blouse   a skirt   shoes   a T-shirt   jeans

socks   slippers   boots   a sweater   pajamas

Ask and answer.

What's | he | wearing?
       | she |

He's | wearing a blue shirt.
She's |

What are they wearing?

They're wearing sweaters and boots.

Yes or no? Ask questions about the pictures above.

Is | he | wearing red slippers?
   | she |

Yes, | he | is.
     | she |

No, | he | isn't.
    | she |

Are they wearing boots?

Yes, they are.

No, they aren't.

What about you?

What are you wearing today?

Let's Read

It's raining.

It's snowing.

The sun is shining.

The wind is blowing.

Playing Outside

The sun is shining. Ann is wearing shorts and a T-shirt. She is climbing a tree.

The wind is blowing. Sue and Jim are wearing jackets. They are flying kites.

It's snowing. Dan and Kim are wearing coats and mittens. They are throwing snowballs.

It's raining. Tim has an umbrella. He is wearing yellow boots. He is jumping in a puddle.

Read and answer.

1. What is Ann wearing?
2. Are Sue and Jim throwing snowballs?
3. What are Dan and Kim doing?
4. What does Tim have?

Sounds and Sentences

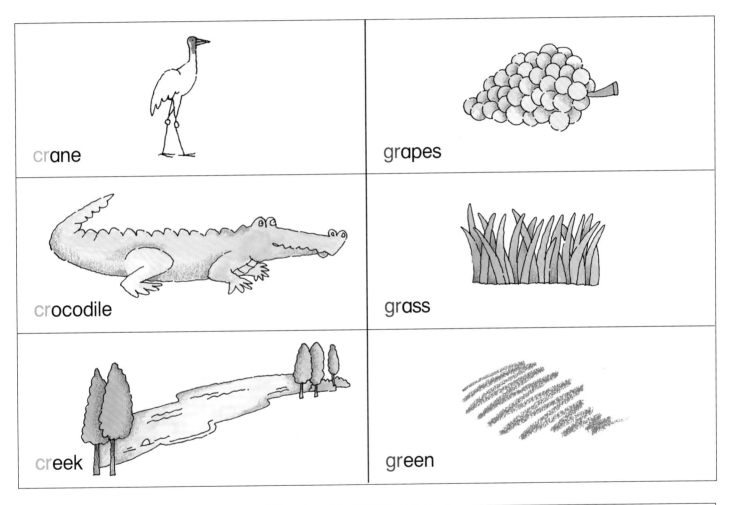

crane

grapes

crocodile

grass

creek

green

A crane and a crocodile are near a creek.

The green grapes are in the green grass.

Let's Sing

♪ Short Shorts ♪

Short shorts, today, they're wearing short shorts today.
The girls are all wearing long jackets,
White T-shirts, black socks,
And short shorts. (short shorts)

Jackets, today, they're wearing jackets today.
The boys are all wearing long jackets,
Black T-shirts, white socks,
And short shorts. (short shorts)

T-shirts, today, they're wearing T-shirts today.
The kids are all wearing long T-shirts,
Long jackets, long socks,
And short shorts. (short shorts)

44

Unit 5

Let's Listen

Listen and circle.

1.
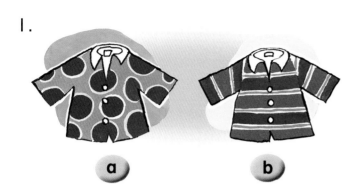

a   b

2.

a   b

3.

a   b

4.
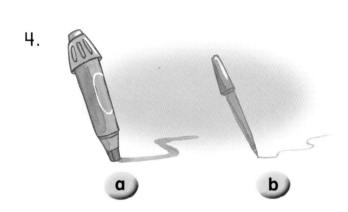

a   b

True or false? Listen and check.

1. ☐ True

   ☐ False

2. ☐ True

   ☐ False

3. ☐ True

   ☐ False

4. ☐ True

   ☐ False

Let's Talk

Let me help you.
Thanks.

Thanks for helping me.
You're welcome.

Ask and answer.

> Where are you going?
> I'm going to the park.

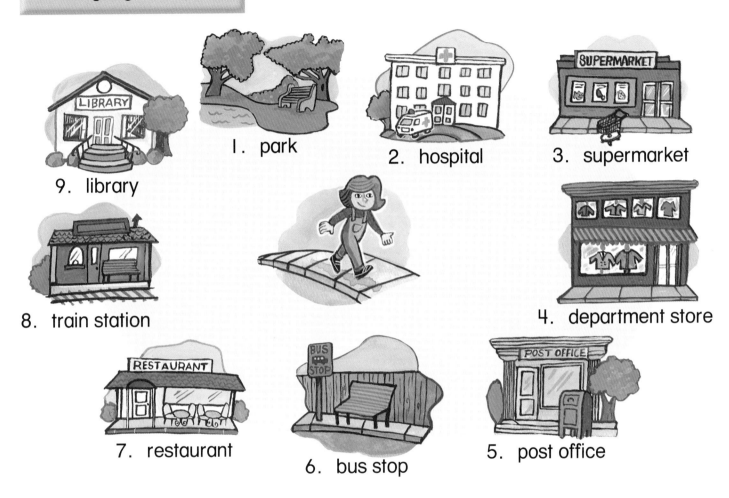

9. library

1. park

2. hospital

3. supermarket

8. train station

4. department store

7. restaurant

6. bus stop

5. post office

Say these.

We're going to the park.

We're going to school.

We're going home.

we are = we're

Unit 6

47

Wendy's riding a bicycle. She's going to the park.

Ben's taking a train. He's going to the library.

Ben's mother is driving a car. She's going to the department store.

Amy and David are walking. They're going to school.

Transportation

walk

take a bus

drive a car

ride a bicycle

take a taxi

take a train

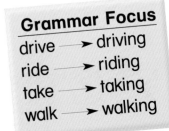

Grammar Focus

drive → driving

ride → riding

take → taking

walk → walking

Ask and answer.

1.
2.
3.
4.
5.
6.

Yes or no? Ask questions about the picture above.

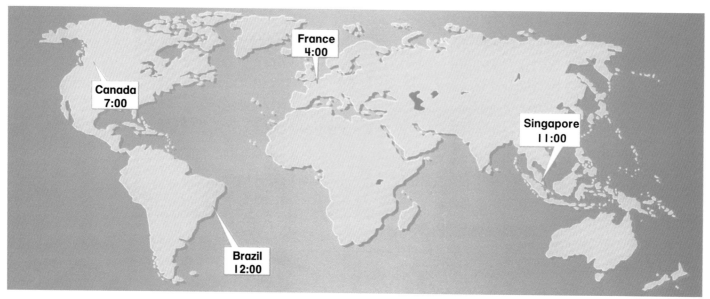

What Are They Doing?

Sally lives in Canada. In Canada it is 7:00 in the morning. Sally is waking up.

Marta lives in Brazil. In Brazil it is 12:00 noon. Marta is eating lunch at school.

Pierre and Marie live in France. In France it is 4:00 in the afternoon. Pierre and Marie are playing outside.

Li-Ping lives in Singapore. In Singapore it is 11:00 at night. Li-Ping is sleeping.

Read and answer.

1. Where does Sally live?
2. What time is it in Brazil?
3. What are Pierre and Marie doing?
4. Does Li-Ping live in Singapore?

Sounds and Sentences

friend

flag

frog

fly

fruit

flower

The frog is eating my friend's fruit.

There is a fly on the flower near the flag.

Let's Sing

♪ The Bookstore Song ♪

Where are you going?
　　To the bookstore.
　　To the bookstore.
　　To the bookstore.
When are you going to the bookstore?
　　We're going there today.

What do you do in the bookstore?
In the bookstore?
In the bookstore?
What do you do in the bookstore?
What do you do each day?

We always look at the books in the bookstore.
In the bookstore.
In the bookstore.
Look at the books in the bookstore.
Look at the books all day.

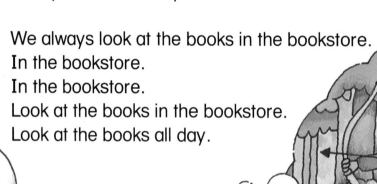

Let's Listen

Listen and circle.

1.

    a   b

2.

    a   b

3.

    a   b

4.

    a   b

5.

    a   b

6.

    a   b

Yes or no? Listen and check.

1. ☐ Yes, he is.

   ☐ No, he isn't.

2. ☐ Yes, she is.

   ☐ No, she isn't.

3. ☐ Yes, they are.

   ☐ No, they aren't.

Let's Review

A. Say and act.

Which hat do you like?

_____.

_____?

No, the big one.

_____.

Thank you.

See you later, Wendy.

_____. Thanks for helping me.

_____.

B. Ask your partner.

Which _____ do you like?

1.

2.

3.

4.

C. Answer the question.

What are you wearing today?

D. Listen and circle.

1.

   a   b

2.

   a   b

3.

   a   b

4.

   a   b

E. Listen and read.

1. Ben is taking a   bus / taxi   to the train station.

2. Amy and David are going to the   supermarket. / department store.

3. Wendy is   walking / running   to the bus stop.

4. David's father is   driving a car / riding a bicycle   to the post office.

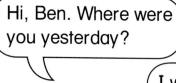

Let's Talk

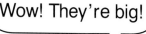

How was it?
It was great.

Ask and answer.

> Where were you yesterday?
>   I was at the beach.
> How was it?
>   It was great.

1. beach

2. museum

3. playground

4. zoo

5. swimming pool

6. amusement park

What about you?

Where were you yesterday? How was it?

Let's Learn

David was on the swing.

Now he's on the slide.

David was on the slide.

Now he's on the seesaw.

David and Wendy were on the seesaw.

Now they're on the jungle gym.

Grammar Focus

is, am ⟶ was

are ⟶ were

58

Ask and answer.

Where was | he?
        | she?

He | was on the jungle gym.
She |

Where is | he | now?
       | she |

He's | on the slide.
She's |

Where were they?

They were on the seesaw.

Where are they now?

They're on the jungle gym.

Yes or no? Ask questions about the picture above.

Was | he | on the slide?
     | she |

Yes, | he | was.
      | she |

No, | he | wasn't.
    | she |

Were they on the seesaw?

Yes, they were.

No, they weren't.

was not = wasn't
were not = weren't

What Was It?

These are very tall trees. They have yellow leaves. What were they before?

This is a black and orange butterfly. It has wings and it can fly. What was it before?

This is a big green frog. It has long legs and it can swim. What was it before?

These are very big flowers. They have yellow petals. What were they before?

| tadpole | caterpillar | seeds | buds |

Make sentences.

1. The trees were _____.
2. The frog was a _____.
3. The flowers were _____.
4. The butterfly was a _____.

Sounds and Sentences

chalk

ship

chair

shopkeeper

teacher

shop

The teacher's chalk is on the chair.

The shopkeeper has a ship in her shop.

♪ Where Were You at Two? ♪

Where were you at two?
    I was at the zoo.
Where were you at three?
    I was in a tree.
Where were you at four?
    We were at the store.
Where were you at five o'clock?
    I was on a great big rock.

Where was he at two?
    He was at the zoo.
Where was she at three?
    She was in a tree.
Where were they at four?
    They were at the store.
Where was Jack? Where was Ray?
    They were here all day.

Let's Listen

True or false? Listen and check.

1. ☐ True
   ☐ False

2. ☐ True
   ☐ False

3. ☐ True
   ☐ False

4. ☐ True
   ☐ False

Listen and circle.

1.

   a   b

2.

   a   b

3.

   a   b

4.

   a   b

Let's Talk

Let's give it to the teacher.
    Good idea.

Ask and answer.

| What did | he
she
they | find? | He
She
They | found a bat. |

Where was it?
It was under a tree.

Grammar Focus
find ⟶ found
do, does ⟶ did

1.
2.
3.
4.
5.
6.

Yes or no? Ask questions about the pictures above.

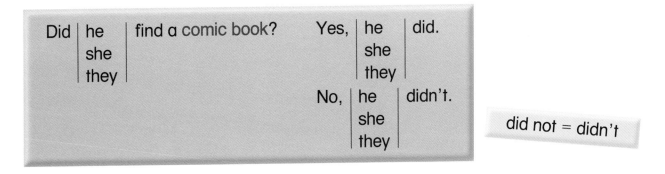

| Did | he
she
they | find a comic book? | Yes, | he
she
they | did. |
| | | | No, | he
she
they | didn't. |

did not = didn't

Let's Learn

Wendy went to the circus yesterday. She saw tigers and elephants.
She ate french fries and cotton candy. She drank lemonade. It was fun.

More Words

monkeys

bears

ice cream

popcorn

soda pop

water

Ask and answer.

What did | he | see?
         | she |
He | saw monkeys.
She |

What did they drink?

They drank soda pop.

What about you?

I had a great day yesterday. I went to the _____. I saw _____. I ate _____.
I drank _____. It was _____!

Last Saturday

Last Saturday Alan went to a museum. He saw rockets and airplanes. He took these pictures.

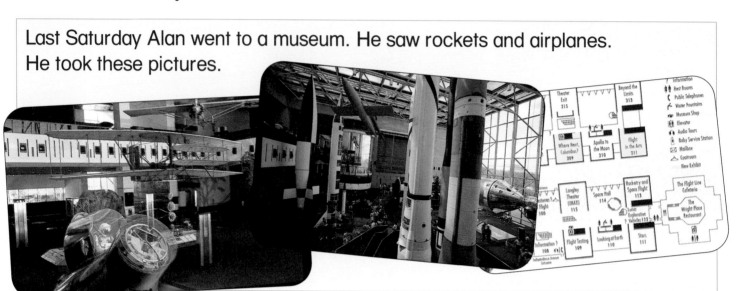

Last Saturday Joy went to an amusement park. She went on a roller coaster. She ate a hot dog and some french fries. She took these pictures.

Last Saturday Jim and Sue went to the beach. They went swimming and had a picnic. They found seashells. They took these pictures.

Read and answer.

1. Where did Alan go last Saturday?
2. What did Joy do at the amusement park?
3. When did Jim and Sue go to the beach?
4. Did they find any seashells?

Sounds and Sentences

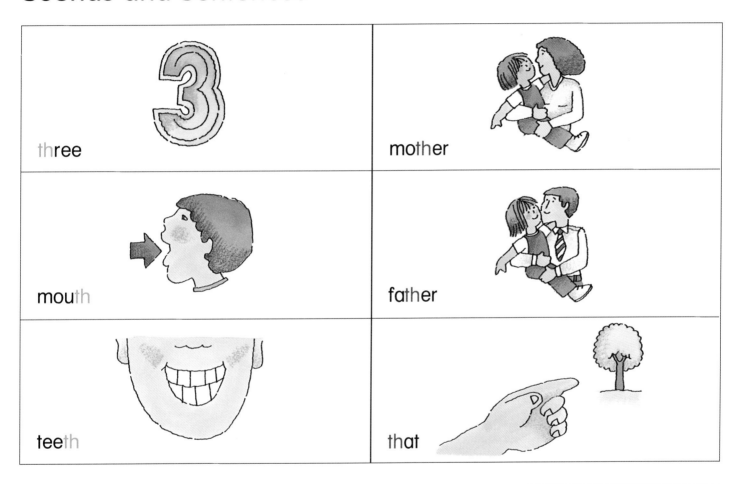

three

mother

mouth

father

teeth

that

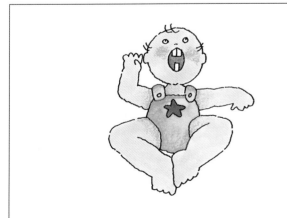

He has three teeth in his mouth.

Her mother and father are by that tree.

Let's Sing

♪ **Where Did You Go?** ♪

Where did you go?
    I went to L.A.
Who did you see?
    I saw Uncle Ray.
What did he do?
What did he say?
    He said, "Good-bye, have a nice day."

What did you drink?
    A cup of tea.
What did you find?
    I found a flea.
What did you eat?
    I ate some fish.
How was the fish?
    It was delicious.

Who did you see?
    My Aunt Marie.
When did you go?
    I went at three.
What did you do?
What did you say?
    I said, "Good-bye, have a nice day."
    When she said, "Hi," I said, "Good-bye,
    Have a nice day. Have a nice day."

Let's Listen

Listen and circle.

1.

    a   b

2.
    a   b

3.
    a   b

4.
    a   b

True or false? Listen and check.

FOOD and DRINKS

1. ☐ True   2. ☐ True   3. ☐ True   4. ☐ True

  ☐ False   ☐ False   ☐ False   ☐ False

Let's Review

A. Say and act.

1. _____? I was at the museum. How was it? _____.

2. I found a wallet. _____? It was under the slide. Let's give it to the teacher. _____.

B. Answer the question.

Where were you yesterday? How was it?

C. Listen and check.

1.

a   b

2.
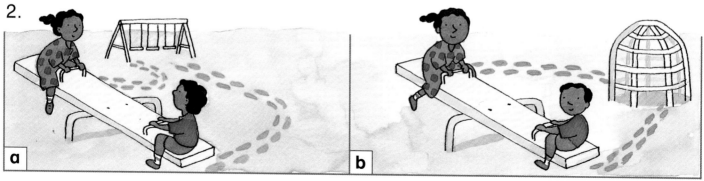

a   b

D. Play a game. Ask and answer.

Where did you go?
What did you eat?
What did you drink?
What did you find?

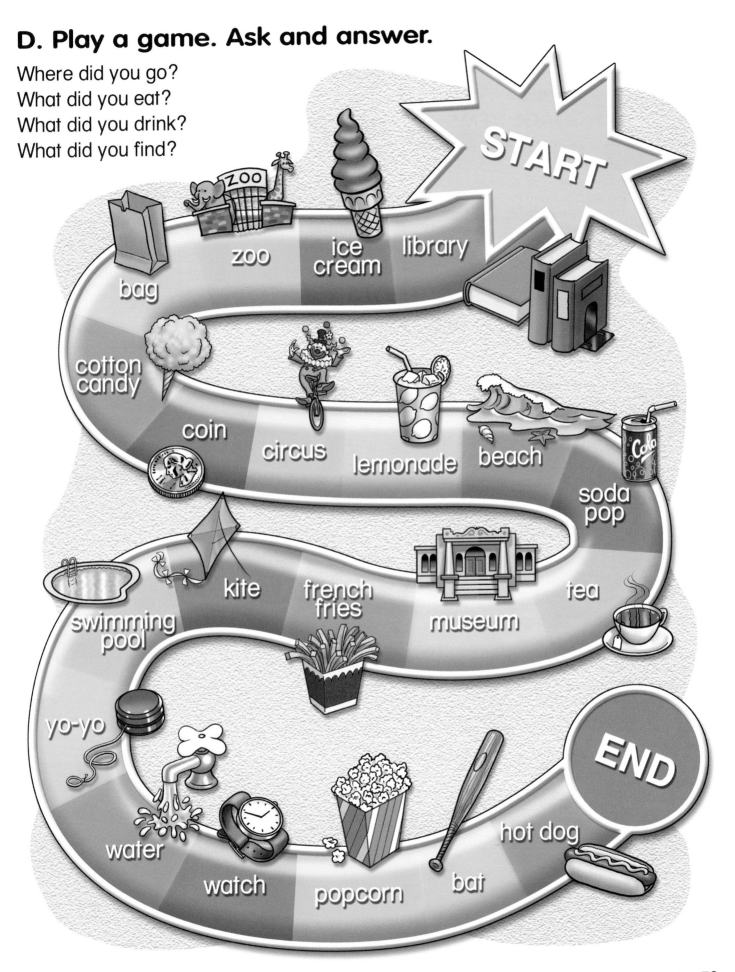

Let's Go 3 Syllabus

UNIT	LANGUAGE ITEMS	FUNCTIONS	TOPICS
1	Excuse me. Where's the (lunchroom)? It's (across from) the (gym). These are my friends, (Ben) and (Wendy). Where is (she)? (She's) in the (music room). (She's) (playing the piano).	Interrupting someone Asking about the location of a place Describing the location of a place Introducing someone Asking where someone is Describing where someone is Describing what someone is doing	Rooms in a school Activities Numbers 1–100
2	What do you have? I have some (paper)? Do you have any (paper)? Yes, I do. No, I don't. Do you want some? Yes, please. No, thanks. What (does she) have? (She has) some (glue). (She doesn't) have any (tape). They have some (tape). They don't have any (paper). (Do they) have any (glue)? Yes, (they do). No, (they don't).	Asking for / offering something Accepting / refusing something Asking about possession (non-count nouns) Expressing possession (non-count nouns)	Classroom objects Shapes
3	Can you play with us tomorrow? Sorry, I can't. I'm busy (every Saturday). Yes, I can. I'm free. What do you do on (Monday)? I go to (art) class. Do you (go to school) on (Sunday)? Yes, I do. No, I don't. What (does she) do after school? (She) (watches TV). (Do they) (watch TV) after school? Yes, (they do). No, (they don't).	Invitations Accepting / refusing an invitation Asking about activities Describing activities	Days of the week Activities
4	I'm sorry I'm late. That's OK. What time is it? It's (three fifteen). When (does he) (get up)? (He) (gets up) at (6:30). (Do they) ever (eat pizza)? Yes, (they) (always) (eat pizza). No, (they) (never) (eat pizza).	Asking about the time Stating the time Asking about daily routine Describing daily routine	Time Frequency Daily activities (review)

UNIT	LANGUAGE ITEMS	FUNCTIONS	TOPICS
5	Which (hat) do you like? I like the (white) one. Do you mean this one? Yes, I do. No, the (big) one. What('s he) wearing? (He's) wearing (a blue shirt). (Are they) wearing (boots)? Yes, (they are). No, (they aren't).	Asking about preferences Expressing preferences Asking for clarification Asking what someone is wearing Describing what someone is wearing	Adjectives Clothes Weather
6	Let me help you. Thanks. Thanks for helping me. You're welcome. Where are you going? I'm going to the (supermarket). Where('s she) going? (She's) going to the (park). How('s she) going there? (She's) (walking). (Are they) going to the (train station)? Yes, (they are). No, (they aren't).	Offering help Asking about a destination Describing a destination Asking about mode of transportation Describing mode of transportation	Places in a community Transportation Countries
7	Where were you yesterday? (I was) at the (beach). How was it? It was (great). Where (was he)? (He was) on the (jungle gym). Where('s he) now? (He's) on the (slide). (Were they) on the (seesaw)? Yes, (they were). No, (they weren't).	Asking about the past Talking about the past	Places to visit Playground equipment Nature
8	Let's give it to the teacher. Good idea. What did (she) find? (She) found a (bat). Where was it? It was (under) (a tree). Did (they) find (a bat)? Yes, (they) did. No, (they) didn't. What did (she) (see)? (She) (saw) (monkeys).	Asking about the past Describing the past Making a suggestion Agreeing with a suggestion	Personal, everyday objects (review) Day trips

Word List

A

a 4
about 20
across from 2
after 22
afternoon 50
again 34
airplane 15
all 34
always 30
amusement
  park 57
an 14
and 2
any 10
are 2
aren't 41
art class 21
at 22
ate 66

B

bag 73
balloon 15
basketball 24
bat 73
beach 57
bears 66
before 60
bicycle 32
big 38
bike 30
bird 16
black 15, 44
blouse 40
blow 15
blowing 42
blue 15, 16
boo hoo 16
books 52
bookstore 23
boots 40
boys' room 3
Brazil 50
brother 25
brown 25
brush 25
brushing 25

buds 60
bus 48
bus stop 47
busy 20
but 12
butterfly 60
by 6
bye 28

C

can 20
Canada 50
can't 20
car 48
caterpillar 60
chair 61
chalk 61
circle 9
circus 66
class 21
classroom 3, 7
clean 7
climbing 42
clock 7
coat 40
coin 73
come 2
come on 64
computer
  class 21
corner 14
cotton candy 66
count 6
crane 43
creek 43
crocodile 43
cup 70

D

day 22
delicious 70
department
  store 47
did 65
didn't 65
dinner 28
dinosaurs 56
do 10
does 13

doesn't 12
dog 14
doing 5
don't 10
drank 66
draw 14, 33
dress 33, 38
drink 66
drive 48
driving 48
drum 33

E

each 52
ear 14
early 32
eat 28
eating 50
eats 31
eight 34
eighteen 6
elephants 66
eleven 6
English class 21
evening 32
ever 31
every 20
excuse 2
eyes 14

F

false 9
family 32
father 24, 69
favorite 24
feeling 16
fifteen 6
fifty 19
find 64
fish 70
five 62
flag 51
flea 70
flower 10, 60
fly 51, 60
flying 42
fold 14
found 64
four 29

fourteen 6
France 50
free 20
french fries 66
Friday 21
friend 51
friends 2
frog 51, 60
from 2
fruit 51
fun 56

G

gave 64
get up 29
gets up 29
girl's room 3
give 64
giving 25
glass 7
glove 7
glue 7, 11
go 20
goes 22
going 46
good 64
good-bye 70
grandmother's
  20
grapes 43
grass 43
great 20
green 10, 43
gym 2

H

had 67
hair 25
happy 16
has 12
hats 38
have 10
he 4
help 46
helping 46
her 8
here you are 10
here 40
he's 4

hey 64
hi 2
him 8
his 22
home 24
homework 21
hospital 47
hot dog 68
house 20
how 49
hungry 28

I

I 10
ice cream 66
idea 64
I'm 2
in 4
is 2
isn't 16
it 14
it's 2

J

jeans 40
jumping 42
jungle gym 58

K

karate class 24
kites 42

L

large 39
last 68
late 28
later 46
learning 16
leaves 60
legs 60
lemonade 66
let 46
let's 12
library 3, 47
live 50
lives 50
long 39

look 38
lunch 35
lunchroom 2

M

making 10
math class 21
me 2
mean 38
minutes 34
mittens 42
Monday 21
monkeys 66
morning 32
mother 48, 69
mouth 69
museum 57
music room 3
my 2

N

name 2
nap 23
near 33
never 30
new 39
next to 3
nice 70
night 32
nineteen 6
no 10
noon 50
nose 14
not 26
now 8
number 9
numbers 6

O

o'clock 29
office 3
oh 20
OK 2
old 39
on 7
one 38
one hundred 6
orange 60
outside 23

P

paint 11
pajamas 40
paper 10
park 47
petals 60
piano 4
piano class 21
picnic 68
pictures 56
pizza 31
plate 15
play 15, 20
playground 57
playing 4, 50
plays 22
please 7
polka-dot 39
popcorn 66
post office 46
practice 22
practices 22
present 25
prince 25
princess 25
puddle 42
purple 38

Q

quarter after 34

R

raining 42
reading 5
really 64
rectangle 14
red 39
restaurant 47
ribbon 11
ride 48
rides 30
riding 48
right 8
rock 62
rockets 68
roller coaster 68
running 55

S

said 70
Saturday 20
saw 66
say 70
school 19
scissors 11
seashells 68
see 20
seeds 60
seesaw 58
seventeen 6
share 12
she 4
she's 4
shining 42
ship 61
shirt 40
shoes 40
shop 61
shopkeeper 61
short 39
shorts 40
sing 16
Singapore 50
sings 22
sister 24
sixteen 6
skirt 40
sleep 31
sleeping 50
slide 58
slippers 40
small 39
snowballs 42
snowing 42
soccer 22
socks 40
soda pop 66
some 10
sometimes 30
song 34
sorry 10
square 14
stays 24
store 62
string 11
striped 39
students 19
studies 22
study 22
sun 42

Sunday 20
supermarket 47
sweater 40
swim 60
swimming 5
swimming
   class 21
swimming
   pool 57
swing 58

T

tadpole 60
tag 31
take 22
takes 22
taking 48
talk 16
tall 60
tape 11
taxi 48
tea 70
teacher 61, 64
teeth 69
tell 34
ten 34
tennis 22
tens 6
thank you 10
thanks 10
that 69
that's 28
the 2
then 22
there 7
these 2
they 4
they're 4
thick 39
thin 39
thirteen 6
this 2
three 69
throwing 42
Thursday 21
tigers 66
time 28
to 6
today 41
tomorrow 20
too 14
took 68

train 33, 48
train station 47
tree 33, 42
triangle 14
truck 33
true 9
T-shirt 40
Tuesday 21
TV 21
twelve 6
twenty 6
two 14

U

umbrella 42
under 64
us 20
usually 30

V

very 26
video 4
video games 23

W

wake up 35
waking up 50
walk 48
walking 48
walks 30
wallet 64
want 10
was 56
wasn't 59
watch 21
watches 22
watching 4
water 66
we 12
wearing 40
Wednesday 21
went 66
were 56
we're 47
weren't 59
what 5
what's 2
when 28
where 3
where's 2

which 38
white 38
who's 8
wind 42
wings 60
with 2
wow 56

Y

yellow 39
yes 10
yesterday 56
you 10
you're welcome
   46
yo-yo 73

Z

zoo 57